UNWAVERING

PRESENTED TO

_____

BY

_____

DATE

_____

Lifeway Press®
Brentwood, Tennessee

ISBN 978-1-4300-9526-2
Item 005847592
Dewey Decimal Classification Number: 242
Subject Heading: DEVOTIONAL LITERATURE / BIBLE STUDY AND TEACHING / GOD

Printed in the United States of America.

Student Ministry Publishing
Lifeway Resources
200 Powell Place, Suite 100
Brentwood, Tennessee 37027

We believe that the Bible has God for its author; salvation for its end; truth, without any mixture of error, for its matter; and that all Scripture is totally true and trustworthy. To review Lifeway's doctrinal guideline, please visit https://www.lifeway.com/about/doctrinal-guidelines.

---

publishing team

Director, Next Gen Ministries
Chuck Peters

Manager, Small Group Resources
Karen Daniel

Writer
Mike Lovato

Content Editor
Kyle Wiltshire

Production Editor
April-Lyn Caouette

Cover Designer
Shiloh Stufflebeam

Graphic Designer
Lisa Olian

TABLE OF CONTENTS

INTRO

We used to play a game on the playground in elementary school called "Red Rover." It's probably illegal now—it was super dangerous. The game had two teams in parallel lines facing each other. Everyone would hold hands across their line, and one team would chant, "Red Rover, Red Rover, send *(the name of someone on the other team)* over." The person whose name was called would leave her team's line, run across toward the other line, and attempt to break through the linked arms (this is where people usually got injured). The defending team would attempt to stand firm and hold strong against the runner who came across. If the runner broke through, she would take someone from the defending team back to her team. Otherwise, she would join the new team she just ran towards.

As Christians, the world we live in has truth under assault. We're like the defending team in "Red Rover," attempting to stand firm while our enemy—Satan—hurls lies at us, striving to knock us down or break us apart. Truth in our culture may seem like a moving target, but God has a different view. Truth is unwavering and we are called as followers of Christ to stand firm in it. It's easier to cave in. It may seem simpler to just let the lies break through and join in with the louder voices. But God is challenging you not to give in and to learn what it means to be unwavering in the truth.

Over the next thirty days, you'll have the opportunity to explore what truth is all about. First, we'll look at some basic elements we know are true. Then, we'll spend some time discovering how the Bible is true. Finally, we'll wrap it up by thinking about how we live in truth as part of our daily lives. Let's dive in and look at how we can live unwavering lives that stand firm in the truth!

GETTING STARTED

This devotional contains thirty days of content, broken down into sections. Each day is divided into three elements—**discover**, **delight**, and **display**—to help you grow in your relationship with God.

DISCOVER

This section helps you examine the Bible in light of who God is and determine what it says about your identity in relationship to Him. Included here is the daily Bible reading and key verses, along with illustrations and commentary to guide you as you learn more about God's Word.

DELIGHT

In this section, you'll be challenged by questions and activities that help you see how God is alive and active in every detail of His Word and your life.

DISPLAY

Here's where you take action. This section calls you to apply what you've learned through each day.

Each day also includes a prayer activity at the conclusion of the devotion.

Throughout the devotional, you'll also find extra items to help you connect with the topic of the book personally, such as Scripture memory verses and interactive articles.

WHAT WE KNOW IS TRUE

WATER IS WET. THE SKY IS BLUE. THERE ARE SOME THINGS IN LIFE WE JUST KNOW TO BE TRUE—AND THERE ARE SOME BASIC TRUTHS AS CHRISTIANS THAT WE CAN SIMPLY AND WHOLEHEARTEDLY BELIEVE. THESE ESSENTIAL REALITIES FORM THE FOUNDATION OF OUR LIVES. WE ALL BUILD OUR LIVES ON SOMETHING. THE FOUNDATIONS WE BASE OUR LIVES ON WILL SHAPE OUR CHARACTER AND OUR ACTIONS.

DAY 1

A SIMPLE YET POWERFUL TRUTH

READ JOHN 3:1-21.

"For God loved the world in this way: He gave his one and only Son,
so that everyone who believes in him will not perish but have eternal life.
For God did not send his Son into the world to condemn the world,
but to save the world through him."
— John 3:16-17

DISCOVER

The most important truth you can ever know is the simple reality that God loves you. How do you know He loves you? You can know He loves you because He chose to give His Son for you. The Father sent Jesus into this world so that people would not die but would receive eternal life.

Many people in our world think that Christians—and therefore God—are simply looking to condemn them. People think that God is in some way watching from above, waiting for them to mess up so that He can tell them what massive failures they are. This couldn't be further from the truth! God didn't send Jesus into the world to be the bearer of bad news and condemnation. God sent Him into the world as the good news: through Him we are able to be saved and have eternal life.

Most parents would find it unthinkable to give up their own child for the sake of someone else. They might be willing to sacrifice themselves, but never to give up the life of their child. God's love for people is so great that He was willing to go through the tremendous sacrifice of giving up His only Son so that people could be brought into a right relationship with Him and experience eternal life.

Why does God's sending Jesus into the world demonstrate His love for all people?

Why do you think some people believe that God sent Jesus into the world to condemn it?

Why is it important for us to fully understand the truth of God's love for us?

DISPLAY

God's love for you is the real deal. He demonstrated it by sending Jesus. You may need to accept and understand this love for the very first time and trust in Jesus to be Your Savior. Perhaps the love God has for you has never really felt like a real thing until you saw it in the Bible today. If this is you, place your faith in Jesus today.

Or maybe you already know Jesus, and today's devotion makes you think about someone in your life who doesn't know about this love yet. Seek out and pray for an opportunity in the next few days to have a gospel conversation with this individual so that he or she can also experience true love.

In your prayer time, spend some time thanking God for the love He has shown you in Jesus. Praise Him that He is love. Love is a key attribute of God's character and who He is. Ask Him to give you a greater understanding of His love so that you can walk securely with Him. Ask Him to give you a heart to find others who need to experience this love.

DAY 2

GOD IS GOOD

READ PSALM 100.

For the Lord is good, and his faithful love endures forever;
his faithfulness, through all generations.
— Psalm 100:5

DISCOVER

How could God let that happen? Have you ever heard someone ask that question? Maybe you've even asked it yourself. We sometimes take credit for the good things that happen in our lives but blame God when bad things happen. We probably can't answer all our questions about the bad things that happen in our world, but there is one simple truth we can cling to during it all: God is good.

The reality of God's goodness is one of the most encouraging things to remember about His character. Imagine a powerful God who is *not* good. It's a terrifying thought. But the one true God, who has revealed Himself through the Bible, is good. So we can remind ourselves of God's goodness even when we don't understand what's going on in our lives, our relationships, or our world.

God's goodness is shown through His faithful love, which the psalmist describes as a love that endures forever. God's love never gives up and will never end. His love continues pursuing us, even in those moments when we feel like giving up. The most beautiful part of God's love is how it's displayed through the Father sending Jesus into this world so that we can be saved from our sin and brought into a right relationship with God. Is there anything better than a perfect God displaying His love to truly imperfect people?

11
UNWAVERING

How does this psalm focus worship on God's goodness?

What does it mean for God to be good?

Why is it powerful to realize that God's faithful love endures forever?

DISPLAY

It's one thing to say God is good, but it's another to get specific about it. Create a list of all the ways you have seen God's goodness in your life. Get creative as you think about it and try to come up with as many examples as you can. Once you've created this list, circle three things you put on the list. Now, think of one person you can tell about the things you circled. It might be a Christian friend or family member. Or maybe you can use one of those items to start a gospel conversation with a friend who doesn't know Jesus yet.

Psalm 100 is a perfect model for how we can praise God. Take some time in prayer to praise Him in the quietness of this moment. Use the different verses in the psalm to help you focus on who God is and how you can praise Him.

HUMAN AND DIVINE

READ JOHN 1:1-18.

The Word became flesh and dwelt among us. We observed his glory, the glory as the one and only Son from the Father, full of grace and truth.
— John 1:14

DISCOVER

We know it's true that Jesus is both fully God and fully human. The Bible shows us places where Jesus revealed His humanity—weeping, eating, and grow tired. The Bible also tells us that Jesus is God Himself. He has power over nature and the ability to forgive sin. He has always existed and will exist forever.

If Jesus were only God, but not human, there would be a few problems: He would not be able to identify with our temptation to sin. He would not be able to stand in our place as a sacrifice for our sins. He would not be able to understand what we're going through. At the same time, if Jesus were only a man, there would be some other problems: He wouldn't be able to be completely perfect and sinless. He wouldn't be able to save us, because only God can save. He wouldn't be worthy of our worship.

Jesus fully understands our experiences as human beings. He's also able to fully save us from our sin. It's an incredible reality that Jesus would come to this earth and take on human flesh. He is one person with two natures: both human *and* divine. This is a truth we can cling to at the core of our faith as Christians.

Who is the "Word" referring to in this passage? How do you know?

What is most meaningful to you about Jesus being fully human?

What is most meaningful to you about Jesus being fully God?

DISPLAY

Today's Scripture tells us that Jesus came and dwelled among us. He lived among people and made His home here. Making your home with people means getting up close with them. Spend some time reflecting and journaling about how Jesus has gotten close to you. Has He brought hope and healing to part of your life? Has He confronted you with areas of sin you needed to deal with? Reflect on some areas where He may be currently working in your life and how He may want you to take some next steps.

Isn't it great that God sent Jesus into this world? Use your time of prayer to thank God for the reality of Jesus being both fully God and fully human. First, praise Him for the beauty of His divinity. Next, thank Him for the aspects of His humanity that mean the most to you. Close your time by asking God to help you show others a clear picture of who Jesus is.

DAY 4

NOT SO PERFECT

READ ROMANS 3:9-26.

For all have sinned and fall short of the glory of God.
— Romans 3:23

DISCOVER

My very first car was quite entertaining. It was about nine years old when I bought it and it had zero upgraded features. No power windows, power locks, or even power steering. It had a cassette tape deck (yes, it was old), a wooden block the previous owner had installed for a fake "eject" button, and a metal coat hanger that had been placed for an antenna. It had no air conditioning and hot vinyl seats. And, last but not least, if you drove faster than sixty-five miles per hour, the steering wheel would start to shake. From time to time, the alignment would get off, which meant that if I took my hands off the steering wheel, the car would slowly drift to one side or the other. It was quite a ride!

Have you ever noticed that your life has a tendency to drift like my first car? Every one of us has sinned—none of us meet God's holy standard. If unchecked, our lives drift toward sin when they are not aligned with God's ways. Even the person who thinks he or she has everything together is still a sinner. God alone is perfect, and our sinfulness helps us see just how much we need a Savior.

In the verses you read today, what makes you aware of everyone's need for a Savior?

According to these verses, what is the only way someone can be righteous before God?

In what ways is it better for us to be justified (made right with God) by faith instead of by keeping the law?

DISPLAY

Do you ever find areas of your life where you like to act as if you have it all together? All of us can sometimes find ourselves thinking we're better than we really are. Sometimes it can be helpful to go back to the place of remembering what Jesus has saved us from. Grab a piece of paper and write down some of the sins Jesus has saved you from. Include some that are recent, but don't be afraid to include some that go back in time, too. Take a moment to experience the weight of the sin that He carried in your place. Now, crumple up the paper and throw it away as you remember that Jesus's sacrifice was enough to pay for every single thing you wrote on that paper and so much more.

Use your prayer time today as an opportunity to come before God in confession. Ask God to show you any sin you may have present in your life. As God reveals sin to you, confess it to Him and repent of it. Thank Him that He has forgiven you of that sin and no longer holds it against you. Commit yourself to living differently now by the power of the Holy Spirit.

DAY 5

ONE WAY

READ JOHN 14:1-6.

Jesus told him, "I am the way, the truth, and the life.
No one comes to the Father except through me."
— John 14:6

DISCOVER

Imagine you're in the middle of the United States and you're wanting to drive to New York City. You and your friends pile into the car, grab some snacks, and start heading towards the highway. As you move in that direction, you see two signs with two different on-ramps. One sign says "San Francisco" and the other says "New York City." Your friend tells you, "I think you can just pick whichever one you want; they both end up in the same place, no matter what." You would probably think your friend is a little confused. You can't get on a road that says it's heading in one direction and expect to end up in a completely different destination.

Many people today like to say that there are many ways to know God or that there are multiple roads that lead to heaven. But Jesus clearly stated that this is not the case. Thomas, one of Jesus's disciples, spoke up and said that the disciples didn't know the way to where Jesus was going. Jesus plainly told Thomas (and the disciples) that He Himself is the way. A statement like this may seem like it excludes people, but if we are going to follow Jesus as our source of truth, we must deal with the reality of His claim that He is the only way to heaven.

How does believing in God help our hearts not be troubled?

How does it comfort you to know that Jesus is preparing a place for you in heaven?

Have you ever wrestled with the claim that Jesus is the only way to God? How has that shaped your thinking?

DISPLAY

People follow all sorts of "ways" in this life as they seek to discover truth, find meaning, or know God. We get the privilege of helping people discover the only true way to eternal life. Create a list of three to five friends or family members who you are willing to commit to praying for regularly and ask God to give you opportunities to share the gospel with them. The incredible thing about asking God for opportunities to share the gospel is that it's a prayer He loves to answer. He will also give you the words and strength you need when the opportunity shows up.

Now is the time to start praying for the people whose names you wrote down. Ask God to bring circumstances into their lives that would cause them to think about spiritual things. Pray that He would open their hearts to hear the gospel in a fresh way. Ask God for a specific opportunity for a conversation where you can share with them.

TRULY FREE

READ JOHN 8:30-47.

"You will know the truth, and the truth will set you free."
— John 8:32

DISCOVER

Can you imagine how incredible it would have been to have lived at the time of Jesus and heard His teaching with your own ears? People were repeatedly astonished by His claims and His authority. In John 8, Jesus is telling people who He is and how those who believe in Him can be forgiven of their sins. And the people believe! There were many people who decided at that time to put their trust in Jesus. This belief led to Jesus showing them what's next: The proof that someone is truly a disciple of Jesus is that he or she continues by obeying what He taught.

This process of continuing to follow would help Jesus's disciples know the truth of the gospel—a truth that sets people free. This truth means people don't have to be stuck in their sins anymore. The challenge for the people listening to Jesus in John 8 is they didn't fully understand that they were slaves to sin. It's pretty tough to seek out freedom when you don't know that you're enslaved. The good news of the gospel requires people to understand the bad news of being enslaved to sin.

People need to know the truth of their sin to understand the truth that Jesus provides freedom from that sin. Imagine being stuck in a cage and never able to experience the big world outside the cage. The first step to freedom from that cage is realizing that you're stuck. This truth paves the way to be able to experience real freedom. In the same way, Jesus brings freedom from our sin.

Why do you think the Jews who Jesus spoke to in these verses didn't see themselves as enslaved?

How does the truth set us free?

What is a truth about God that you need to know more so you can experience freedom?

DISPLAY

How did you come to know the truth about Jesus? It can be helpful to occasionally reflect on our story of how we first became a Christian. Take time to write out your story of discovering the truth and finding freedom. Grab a piece of paper or a journal. Divide the sheet into three sections, and label them: "My Life Before Jesus," "How I Met Jesus," and "My Life Since Meeting Jesus." Write out your story according to each of these sections, focusing first on life before Jesus (even if you were young). Next write about how you discovered that you needed a Savior and came to know Him. Finally, write about how your life has changed since you met Jesus. Sometimes, it's powerful to share with others about the work God has been doing in our lives recently. Look for an opportunity to share this story with someone else this week.

Even when we know Jesus, we can find ourselves living as if we were a slave to sin again. In your prayer time, ask God to reveal any areas where you may be living as a captive instead of as a free person. Ask God to show you the truth of His love for you once again, and embrace His forgiveness as you repent of your sin.

MEMORY VERSE

MEMORY VERSE

MEMORY VERSE

MEMORY VERSE

MEMORY VERSE

MEMORY VERSE

MEMORY VERSE

> ## WHEN THE SPIRIT OF TRUTH COMES, HE WILL GUIDE YOU INTO ALL THE TRUTH. FOR HE WILL NOT SPEAK ON HIS OWN, BUT HE WILL SPEAK WHATEVER HE HEARS. HE WILL ALSO DECLARE TO YOU WHAT IS TO COME.
>
> — John 16:13

FATHER OF LIES

READ JOHN 8:30-47.

"You are of your father the devil, and you want to carry out your father's desires. He was a murderer from the beginning and does not stand in the truth, because there is no truth in him. When he tells a lie, he speaks from his own nature, because he is a liar and the father of lies."
— John 8:44

DISCOVER

Let's take a look at the same verses we read yesterday but with a different set of eyes. It's a reality of our world that many people don't believe in Jesus. Here, we see the reason why: If God is not someone's Father, it means that person's father is the devil, instead. By nature, because of our sin, people are children of the devil—and it's his desire to keep us that way. People naturally follow what the enemy desires for their lives. The reason Satan can do this so successfully is because he's a deceiver.

The enemy, Satan, primarily attacks people by lying to them. Why? Because being a liar is his very nature. In fact, Jesus calls him the "father of lies." He uses lies to deceive us into sin by making promises that he can't keep. Sin promises to bring you purpose, joy, and fulfillment, but it can never deliver on those promises. Yet people continue to buy into these lies. Jesus provides a stark contrast to the devil. Jesus only speaks truth, and He always delivers on His promises.

What are some ways the devil has lied to you?

How can we fight the lies of the devil?

Why do you think people are so quick to believe lies instead of truth?

DISPLAY

Sin makes promises it can't keep. What are some lies you've believed that the enemy has put out there? Maybe you have believed that the pursuit of more stuff will make you happy. Maybe you believe that sex outside of God's design is going to give you ultimate fulfillment. Or perhaps you believe the core lie that you know better than God does. Whatever lies you have believed, commit to replace them with the truth of God's Word and the gospel. You may find lies occasionally popping into your mind. Intentionally speak truth to yourself in those moments.

Ask God to give you a heart that is soft to truth. Pray that He will help you love things that are true and hate things that are false. Ask God to give you a mind that can quickly understand truth from lies. Submit your thoughts to His ways.

DAY 8

PROMISE KEEPER

READ HEBREWS 6:13-20.

Because God wanted to show his unchangeable purpose
even more clearly to the heirs of the promise, he guaranteed
it with an oath, so that through two unchangeable things, in which it is
impossible for God to lie, we who have fled for refuge might
have strong encouragement to seize the hope set before us.
— Hebrews 6:17-18

DISCOVER

As human beings, it's so easy for us to lie. We lie to cover up our mistakes or sins. We lie so we don't get embarrassed. We lie to make ourselves look better than we are. You don't have to teach a kid to lie—we come into life with that skill completely figured out.

God, on the other hand, is the exact opposite. God is the definition of truth. He never lies. In Hebrews 6, the writer reveals how God showed that He is unchanging in His purpose. It's literally impossible for God to lie.

The truthfulness of God helps us find a place we can take refuge and find hope. In life, we can have a hard time finding a place where we feel safe. It's often difficult for us to trust people. It makes all the difference to know we have a relationship with the God who never breaks our trust. He always keeps His promises. If God has said it, we can trust that He will follow through with it. In a world full of promise breakers, God is the ultimate promise keeper.

What does the fact that God never lies help us realize about the rest of the Bible?

How did God show Himself as a promise keeper to Abraham? (Take a look at Genesis 22 if you need some help.)

Are there any areas in which you struggle to trust that God will keep His promises? What are these areas?

We look to all sorts of places to find refuge and hope in life. Of course, those places often let us down and make us feel emptier than when we started. What would it look like to shift your thinking and look to God as that first place of refuge and hope? Maybe there's an area in your life where you've been struggling to see how God will come through. Write down any areas where it's been a struggle to trust that God will keep His promises from His Word.

In your prayer time, take time to reflect deeply on God's truthfulness. Thank Him for always keeping His promises. Meditate on specific promises you've seen Him keep in your life. Declare to Him that you will trust Him to follow through on His promises even when it seems scary. Depend on Him to be your refuge and hope.

SPIRIT OF TRUTH

READ JOHN 16:7-15.

*"When the Spirit of truth comes, he will guide you into all the truth.
For he will not speak on his own, but he will speak whatever he hears.
He will also declare to you what is to come."*
— John 16:13

DISCOVER

It would be incredible to walk down a beach or through a park with Jesus. It would be amazing to learn from Him and hear directly from Him. His disciples all had that experience as they walked around with Him during His ministry on earth. But then, He told them something absolutely shocking: He told them it would be better for Him to leave. What in the world could He mean? How could it be better for the disciples to be without Jesus physically walking with them?

Jesus claimed it would be better because if He didn't leave, the Holy Spirit couldn't come. The Holy Spirit guides Jesus's disciples into all truth. He did this in the first century as the apostles completed the rest of what we have today as the New Testament, and He also does this today as He guides us into all the truth.

We cannot understand truth on our own—we need the Holy Spirit to open our eyes and hearts to God's truth. So, would you rather walk in person with Jesus or have the Holy Spirit? Jesus said it's better for us to have the Spirit. The Holy Spirit lives inside every follower of Jesus, helping us know truth and empowering us to live for Him.

How do you think the disciples first reacted when Jesus told them it was better for Him to leave?

What roles does the Spirit have according to these verses?

How does it encourage you to know that, as believers, we have the Holy Spirit living inside of us?

DISPLAY

One of the ways the Holy Spirit reveals truth to us is when we hide it in our heart by memorizing Scripture. We can have a powerful set of tools at our disposal when we fill our minds and hearts with Bible verses. Here's what will happen: You memorize Scripture, and then, when you face real-life situations that are beyond your own strength, the Holy Spirit will bring those verses to mind to help you. Start today by memorizing John 16:13. Write it down somewhere you'll see it often, or keep it as a note on your phone, and review it throughout the day.

In your prayer time, ask God to help you hear the voice of the Holy Spirit more clearly. Ask Him to speak to you through the truth of the Bible as you read it each day. Take time to simply listen during this prayer time to what God may be saying to you through the Holy Spirit as He helps you understand the Bible.

DAY 10

GOD IS NEAR

READ PSALM 145.

The LORD is near all who call out to him, all who call out to him with integrity.
— Psalm 145:18

DISCOVER

I'm a dad of two daughters. Sometimes when they were little, they'd get scared at night. I bet you had some nights like that too. In their fear, they'd call out to me and I'd go over to check on them. Some nights, it would just take a couple words to calm them. But other nights, they simply would not let me leave. They needed me in the room. They needed me near. So, I would fall asleep on the floor near their bed and sometimes wake up at 2:30 in the morning to head back to my own comfy bed.

There is something incredible about having someone near who we trust. Many people view God as a far-off being. If they do believe in God at all, they may see Him as a God who created the universe but now stands back at a distance, uninvolved with His creation.

This is not who God is. The truth is that God is near. He is close. Look at your arm and picture how close the air itself is to your skin right now. God is closer than that. It's a wonderful thing to know the God who is not far away but remains near to His children. We can call out to Him at any time and know that He hears us and is close.

Do you tend to view God as near or far away? Why?

What does it look like for you to call out to God?

What are some other truths from Psalm 145 that grab your attention?

DISPLAY

It can sometimes be hard to grasp the reality that God is near. Why? Because we can't see Him. It's easy to know that your friend is in the room when you literally hear your friend's voice or see him or her sitting nearby. But, with God, we sometimes need to be intentional in reminding ourselves that He is near. Find some sticky notes or note cards that you can write on. Write "God is near" on several of them and place them around your room, bathroom, or car. Put them in places where you'll see them frequently. Every time you come across one, take a short pause and remind yourself of that truth you are reading.

Start your prayer time by slowing down. It's a good practice to begin prayer by simply stepping away from the distractions of the day and acknowledging God's presence. As you begin to pray, just say to God, "You are here." As you pray, focus deeply on that truth and talk to God as if He is physically sitting next to you.

GOD'S WORD IS TRUE

THE BIBLE IS TRULY A UNIQUE
BOOK. ITS COLLECTION OF
SIXTY-SIX BOOKS CARRIES A
CONSISTENT MESSAGE ABOUT
WHO GOD IS AND HOW PEOPLE
CAN KNOW HIM. THE MOST
UNIQUE FEATURE OF THE BIBLE
IS THAT IT'S HOW GOD HAS
CHOSEN TO REVEAL HIMSELF
TO PEOPLE. WE DON'T HAVE TO
GUESS THE TRUTH ABOUT GOD.
HE HAS REVEALED TRUTH TO US
THROUGH HIS WORD.

THE TRUE WORD

READ JOHN 17:14-19.

"Sanctify them by the truth; your word is truth."
— John 17:17

DISCOVER

We can see so much about people by what they pray about. Maybe we see a grandmother praying desperately for her grandkids who are making bad choices. A husband might pray intensely for his wife who was just diagnosed with cancer. We see pastors who pray for their congregation that they might seek God more intentionally. So what can we learn from a prayer that Jesus prayed?

John 17 captures a prayer Jesus prayed just before He was betrayed by Judas. In it, Jesus prays in three categories: for Himself, for His disciples, and for all future believers who will follow Him because of the disciples' faith. In this middle category, we see a prayer for Jesus's disciples that includes even us today: He prays that we would be sanctified by the truth, and He states clearly that God's Word is truth. "Sanctify" means to be made holy or set apart. We are made holy by the truth of God's Word.

In other words, it's impossible to say you want to grow as a Christian without spending time in the Bible. The Bible shows us who God is, what He's like, how to know Him, and how to live as His people. As a follower of Jesus, it's important to stay strong in your conviction that God's Word is true. You can base your life firmly on the Bible because it's how God has revealed Himself to us.

What parts of Jesus's prayer stand out most to you? Why?

Why is it significant that Jesus prayed for us to be protected from the evil one rather than for us to be just taken out of the world?

How can we take steps to make sure we are being sanctified by the truth of God's Word?

DISPLAY

How's your intake of the Bible? Many Christians have expressed a desire to grow in their faith and have a stronger walk with Jesus. But those same Christians sometimes don't put in the effort to engage in regular reading, study, or meditation on the Bible. You're not going to go very far in your faith if you're not intentionally spending time in God's Word. Make a plan to get into God's Word. Maybe it's committing to be more consistent using the book in your hand right now. Maybe you need to find a plan through an app on your phone. Or maybe you need to get a friend to help hold you accountable for spending time in the truth of the Word.

Just as Jesus prayed that we would be sanctified by the truth, you can pray the same thing for yourself. Ask God to make you holy by the truth. Ask God to give you an increased hunger for His Word. Commit to hear from God daily through reading the Bible.

UNCHANGING

READ PSALM 119:153-160.

*The entirety of your word is truth, each of
your righteous judgments endures forever.*
— Psalm 119:160

DISCOVER

Outdated and out of touch.

That's what many people today think about the Bible. They see it as an
ancient book that has nothing to do with life today. While it's definitely an
ancient book, the second part is false—the Bible has everything to do with
life today. God's standards don't change. God Himself is eternal, and He
is unchanging. He has spoken to us through His Word and His instructions
are also unchanging. If we see God's Word as out of touch with modern
culture, it's not the Bible that needs to change to catch up—it's us who
need to realign our lives with the eternal truths of Scripture.

Not only is God's Word unchanging, but all of it is true. Another tendency
we have today is to keep the parts of the Bible we like and eliminate the
parts we have trouble agreeing with. It's crucial for us to realize that the
entirety of the Bible is God's truth. We don't get to pick which parts we
want to obey.

The psalmist recognized that a fulfilling life comes from following God's
instructions as found in His Word. Those who don't follow His ways suffer
the consequences. But when we understand that God's instructions are still
relevant today, we can embrace His way of living and experience His work
in our lives.

How does the psalmist respond when he goes through attacks and persecution? What stands out about this response to you?

How should we approach the Bible when modern culture sees it as outdated and irrelevant?

Are there parts of God's Word you tend to ignore and need to pay more attention to? What makes you want to ignore it?

DISPLAY

While our culture might struggle to accept that the Bible hasn't changed over time, we can find rest in that truth. An unchanging Bible means we have an unchanging God who is faithful and trustworthy. You can trust Him and you can trust His Word. It's not going to change as if God was moody and changed His mind. Take some time to journal some reasons of your own that you love God's Word. Write down why you're thankful for it being unchanging and everlasting.

In your prayer time, ask God to help you embrace all of His Word. Thank Him for giving us knowledge of Himself that doesn't change as time goes on. Ask Him to help you learn to obey the parts of His Word that may seem difficult or challenging in today's world.

A HELPFUL WORD

READ 2 TIMOTHY 3:10-17.

All Scripture is inspired by God and is profitable for teaching,
for rebuking, for correcting, for training in righteousness,
so that the man of God may be complete, equipped for every good work.
— 2 Timothy 3:16-17

DISCOVER

Our Bible contains two letters that Paul wrote to his younger student, Timothy. Today's Scripture reading looks at how Timothy had been an incredible companion to Paul and followed him faithfully, learning from Paul's example of faith. And that wasn't easy! Paul pointed out that everyone following Jesus faithfully will be persecuted and deception will continue to grow.

What's the solution? Paul encouraged Timothy (and us) to lean into the truth of the Scriptures. The Bible gives us everything we need for life, both in what we believe and how we live. The Bible helps us clearly see what is true and what is not. God's Word helps us know the right choice to make as well as the wrong choices that we need to avoid.

Scripture is powerful because it is inspired by God Himself. This isn't inspiration like a person being overcome by his or her feelings for someone and writing a love poem. The inspiration Paul is describing is the reality that the Bible was breathed out by God Himself. God used the unique personalities of the writers, guiding them and helping them know what to write. As a result, the Bible is an incredibly practical book. It's not a book just full of old stories or wise sayings. It's a book that helps us live the life God has called us to live and that shapes us into the people God has called us to be.

What are the different elements mentioned in verse 10 that Timothy learned from Paul? Why are these important?

How can God's Word help us face persecution and deception?

How does it make you feel to know that Scripture is inspired by God?

DISPLAY

God's Word isn't abstract—it's helpful to our lives because it comes from God Himself. Take a piece of paper and divide it into four squares. Write the following headings above the different squares: "Teaching," "Rebuking," "Correcting," and "Training for Righteousness." List out ways you see how God's Word can be helpful in your life in each category. For instance, under "Correcting," you might write, "Shows me truths about God that I have misunderstood." Try to list at least two or three items in each square. After you've created these lists, circle one area you can focus on growing in over the next few days.

As you pray today, ask God to help you use His Word in these practical ways. Thank Him for communicating to us through the Bible. Ask Him for direction and strength in your life as you seek to apply His Word in these different ways. Surrender to His instruction through His Word.

DAY 14

AN ENCOURAGING WORD

READ ROMANS 15:1-6.

*For whatever was written in the past was written for our
instruction, so that we may have hope through endurance
and through the encouragement from the Scriptures.*
— Romans 15:4

DISCOVER

Christians don't always agree with each other. Maybe you've seen this up
close. It can be true with politics, general opinions, or even minor areas
of theology. In his letter to the Romans, Paul addressed how Christians
should handle it when immature believers feel strongly about something
that mature believers do not. Paul emphasized that the Christian life isn't
about insisting on getting our own way. Instead, it's about putting the
needs of others ahead of our own.

How do we live in harmony with others? God's Word gives us what we
need. Specifically, we can have hope in our relationships and stand strong
in them because the Bible gives us encouragement. The Bible was written
thousands of years ago, but everything in it is still helpful today. It wasn't
just written to give us interesting stories but to give us instructions for life.
The truth of Scripture helps us in our relationships and in every other area
we face as we go through life.

The result of this encouragement from God's Word is that we live in
harmony with one another. Think about music: We love listening to
instruments that are in harmony with each other. They aren't fighting for
attention or doing their own thing. We also ought to live in harmony with
fellow Christians as we gain encouragement from God's Word.

What are some areas today where weaker Christians might feel differently than stronger Christians?

How can the Scriptures help remind us to endure through difficulties?

How does the Bible bring you encouragement in your relationships?

DISPLAY

Do you have any Christian friends whom you haven't been living in harmony with? If so, decide today to make it right. Search the Scriptures for verses that will encourage you to be a harmonious friend to other believers. Maybe everything is good in your Christian friendships right now. If so, think about how you can continue to be an encouragement to those friends and help bring them together as you journey through life. Find some verses you can text to your friends or send as notes that will encourage them today.

Pray and thank God for the gifts of hope, endurance, and encouragement through His Word. Thank Him for the hope we have because of Jesus. Praise Him for the work that endurance does in your life as it builds your character. Reflect on the encouragement He gives you through the Bible. Ask Him to continue showing you how to live today as He speaks to you through the Bible.

INTENTIONS OF THE HEART

READ HEBREWS 4:12-13.

For the word of God is living and effective and sharper than any double-edged sword, penetrating as far as the separation of soul and spirit, joints and marrow. It is able to judge the thoughts and intentions of the heart.
— Hebrews 4:12

DISCOVER

I love books. I love spending time in libraries, stores with brand-new books, and used bookstores that have a distinctive "old book" smell. A good book has power: It comes alive when you read it. You can picture the story in your mind. You feel the emotions the characters feel.

The Bible comes alive in a completely different way. Yes, it has some of those same characteristics I just mentioned. But, more than that, the Bible has a way of looking inside the heart of the reader. God is the author of Scripture which makes it different than any other book you've ever read. His Spirit speaks through the words of Scripture and brings conviction to each of us in a powerful way.

As God brings you conviction through the Scripture, His goal isn't to make you feel bad and leave you sitting there in that shame. God's purpose in conviction is always to move you to repentance and back to Him. When we read the Bible and it reveals an aspect of our life that needs to change, it's our opportunity to make a change through the power of the Holy Spirit who lives in us.

What are some ways the author of Hebrews describes God's Word in today's verses? Which way stands out to you the most?

How have you seen God's Word judge the thoughts and intentions of your heart?

Verse 13 explains that God knows everything and that we will give an account to Him. How do you think we should respond to this truth?

DISPLAY

Our verses today describe God's Word as a sword that is very precise, almost like a surgeon's scalpel. It's important for us to regularly submit to God's Word as it performs that surgical function in our hearts. Create a list of questions you can ask yourself on a regular basis after reading God's Word to help you see what God may be trying to expose in you. Here's a sample question to get you started: "Does this passage reveal a specific sin I need to repent of?" Another question might be: "Is there a command here I'm not obeying that I need to?"

Today's verses give us a great opportunity to make a prayer of confession. Ask God to reveal areas where His Word has been speaking to you but perhaps you haven't been listening or responding. Repent of what He shows you and make the decision to walk forward in obedience and faithfulness.

A SHINING LIGHT

READ PSALM 119:105-112.

Your word is a lamp for my feet and a light on my path.
— Psalm 119:105

DISCOVER

Have you ever been walking through the woods on a dark night and couldn't see much of anything at all? It can be scary when you're not sure what's in front of you or the next step to take. But light can make all the difference in the world. If you have a lantern with you, you can light up the area around your feet to make sure you don't trip on any tree roots or slip off the side of a path.

If you have a flashlight, you're in an even better situation. You can shine the light down the path to see what's ahead. You can be more aware of dangers ahead that you may need to avoid. You can make adjustments based on what you see around the next corner. The flashlight may even show you when it's best to simply turn around and go a different direction because of the dangers on the path ahead.

God's Word serves as a light in this same way. We face all sorts of difficult situations as we go through life. But God's Word can be an immediate light around us to help see more clearly what we are facing. The Bible shines light ahead to help us know the right direction to go. The key is making sure we turn on the light God provides us so we can use it well in our time of need.

How does seeing God's Word as a lamp and light help us keep our commitments to Him?

What are some situations where you think people your age may need the light of God's Word?

What does it look like to be resolved to obey God's statues (see v. 112)?

DISPLAY

The two pictures of a lamp and light in this passage show us a vision of the Bible helping us see what's immediately surrounding us and what's just down the path. But there's one thing that isn't included in these pictures: Neither of them gives us a long-distance look way into the future. This is where trust comes in. You may think that life would be easier if we could see far out and know what's down the road. But God often simply shows us our next step in our walk following Him rather than a detailed plan. Choose to trust in His ways and follow through on the small next steps He shows you through His Word.

In your prayer time, ask God to shine the light of His Word clearly on the circumstances of your life. Maybe there's a situation you're facing right now where you need some better vision and clarity. Ask God to help you see what He wants you to see.

MEMORY VERSE

"

THE ENTIRETY OF YOUR WORD IS TRUTH, EACH OF YOUR RIGHTEOUS JUDGMENTS ENDURES FOREVER.

— Psalm 119:160

TRUTH AND LIES

READ 2 PETER 3:14-18.

He speaks about these things in all his letters. There are some things hard to understand in them. The untaught and unstable will twist them to their own destruction, as they also do with the rest of the Scriptures.
— 2 Peter 3:16

DISCOVER

The Bible is an incredible book, but it's not always easy to understand. Sometimes we don't have enough knowledge about the culture at the time of its writing to fully grasp what the author was originally saying. Sometimes it's hard to understand because it's difficult to obey. But we shouldn't avoid things just because they are hard. The call to follow Jesus means we must pursue knowing Him through His Word.

Some people take advantage of the Bible being hard to understand and twist it to say something completely different than what it actually means. We probably wouldn't fall for lies and false teaching if they were super obvious. But what happens is that the truth gets twisted into a different version of itself that's no longer true, and the result of this twisting is destruction. A belief in lies never led anyone to know God. This belief leads people away from Him and to destruction.

So it's critical for us to put in the hard work of knowing the Scriptures well. This starts with reading the Bible regularly, but there's more to it than that. This also means learning what you can from your pastor in his sermons. It means finding reliable Bible study tools online and using them to help you study God's Word. It means comparing what you hear people say about the Bible to what you actually read in the Bible.

What are some ways we can seek to be found without spot or blemish (see v. 14)?

How does verse 16 help us see that Paul's writings (which make up a lot of the New Testament) are to be considered as Scripture?

How can we make sure to not be deceived by people who twist and distort the truth of the Bible?

DISPLAY

I recently met a young man in his early twenties who came to our church after realizing he had started getting involved in a cult! He started out just attending what he thought was a regular Bible study. But it started getting a little strange, and when he did some research, he learned all about the group he'd gotten involved with. He jumped out fast! Your mission for today is to do your homework. Not the homework you have in school (although you should do that too), but the homework of seeking truth in a world full of lies. Just because someone says something is true, that doesn't mean it is!

Ask God to give you deeper insight into His Word. Pray that He would help you be able to clearly distinguish truth from lies. Ask God to help you be on guard against this type of error. Seek to understand His truth more fully as you follow Him.

SPIRITUAL NOURISHMENT

READ MATTHEW 4:1-11.

*He answered, "It is written: Man must not live on bread
alone but on every word that comes from the mouth of God."*
— Matthew 4:4

DISCOVER

What do you do when you're tempted? Most of us respond in one of
three ways: The first option is to just give in. We think we can't handle the
temptation and that we have no tools to fight it, so we just cave in. The
second option is to fight the temptation in our own strength. This works . . .
for a little bit. You can resist temptation in your own power sometimes, but
not fully. And usually it ends up really draining you. The third option is to
fight temptation in the strength of the Holy Spirit and with God's Word.
This is how Jesus handled temptation when the devil tempted Him in the
wilderness. Rather than giving in or going on in His own strength, He made
use of the nourishment that comes from God's Word.

The devil threw three temptations at Jesus, and He answered all three of
them by quoting Scripture. This first response in verse 4 gives huge insight
into God's Word. Jesus quotes Deuteronomy 8:3 and helps us see that
our strength doesn't come from physical food but from the spiritual food
we get from God. God feeds us spiritually through the Bible and gives us
the strength to fight temptation. We need that spiritual nourishment every
single day. Just like you can't go a long period of time without eating
physical food, you need spiritual food every day so you have a healthy diet
of God's Word.

What do you think Jesus's physical condition was like by the time He faced this temptation?

What is so powerful about using Scripture to fight temptation?

How can you get more Scripture into your life as you battle against the temptations that come your way?

DISPLAY

When I was a kid, they would try to sell sugary cereals to you in TV commercials by showing how they were healthy and part of a "well-balanced diet." Then they'd cut to a shot of cereal alongside a couple eggs, some fruit, and a tall glass of orange juice—the real well-balanced diet. We need to balance our spiritual nourishment as well. Try not to jump around when you read the Bible but pick plans that will focus you in on a book, a theme, or an aspect of knowing God.

In your prayer time, ask God to remind you of verses you've memorized that will help you fight temptation. If you can't think of any verses you've memorized, pray that God would lead you to some verses to memorize and use as a resource in the fight. Pray that God would protect you against temptation and give you exactly what you need when you need it.

BLINDED

READ 2 CORINTHIANS 4:1-6.

In their case, the god of this age has blinded the minds of the unbelievers to keep them from seeing the light of the gospel of the glory of Christ, who is the image of God.
— 2 Corinthians 4:4

DISCOVER

I sometimes have a hard time finding things in my house. I'll be looking for something in a drawer or on a counter and it seems like I just can't find it. Usually, I'll ask my wife where something is and she'll tell me. It's often the place I've just been looking, so I'll go back in to search some more. Still no luck. Then, my wife comes over and immediately finds the item I've been hunting for. I had been blind to the thing that was right in front of my eyes, but she could see it immediately.

Our enemy, "the god of this age," blinds unbelievers so they can't see the beauty and truth of the gospel, even though it seems so clear to those of us who follow Jesus. God's Word proclaims the good news so clearly, but it gets missed by so many people.

The beauty is that we get to shine light into dark places. We get to shine light on the truth that so many unbelievers are blinded to. Our hope is that they will see through the darkness and see the truth that's been hidden from them. They may have been searching for truth and purpose for some time, but as God's Spirit is at work, we get the opportunity to help them find what they truly need.

What did Paul and his partners in ministry do instead of giving up?

What are some ways people are being blinded to the gospel?

Why is it important to focus on proclaiming Jesus instead of ourselves?

DISPLAY

It can be helpful when you realize the reality that the enemy is actively blinding unbelievers to the gospel. You can't automatically just undo that. But God can remove blinders from people's eyes. He can help them see the truth as He reveals Himself to them by His Spirit and through His Word. The pressure is not on you to try and "save" people. Your job is to pray for people and to clearly proclaim the gospel message, then be ready to help them know Jesus personally when the moment is right. So, make this your prayer today.

Start your prayer time by picturing people in your mind who don't yet know Jesus as their Savior. Ask God to remove the blinders from their eyes. Ask for the Holy Spirit to work in their hearts and break down the hard places. Ask Him for opportunities to share the truth so they can have an opportunity to respond.

ARMOR UP

READ EPHESIANS 6:10-20.

For this reason take up the full armor of God, so that you may be able to resist in the evil day, and having prepared everything, to take your stand.
— Ephesians 6:13

DISCOVER

Imagine enlisting in the military and getting ready to head off to war. You say goodbye to your family and friends, get on a plane, and make your way to a far-off country. When you get there, you head out into battle, but you're still in your civilian clothes. You're wearing a t-shirt, jeans, and some casual shoes. Meanwhile, the enemy you face is armored up and ready to fight.

A battle requires the right clothing and equipment to fight it. Paul gives a picture in Ephesians 6 of the armor of God. We're commanded here to take up this armor so that we're ready to fight in the battles we all face. The armor that Paul lists in this chapter is made up entirely of things that come from God's Word. When he says to put on the shield of faith, he's talking about saving faith and trust that is described in the Bible. So, putting on the armor starts with understanding the different pieces of the armor from Scripture.

We may not know the day the battle is coming, which makes it critical to armor up before it happens. Good soldiers prepare during their training, not once they arrive on the battlefield. The key is at the start of the passage where we are told to be strong, not in our own power but by the strength of the Lord. He provides the strength and the armor for the battle.

Why do you think the devil's plans are described as "schemes" in verse 11?

Which piece of armor do you feel well equipped with? Why?

Which piece do you need more equipping with? Why?

DISPLAY

Armor is useless if it sits on the shelf. You can read all about righteousness, faith, the gospel, and the other pieces mentioned. But if you don't put on those pieces of armor, they're useless. This is why obedience is so important. There are lots of Christians who know a lot of information about the Bible but never live it out as intended. Is there any truth of Scripture you've read recently that you haven't yet followed in obedience? Decide today to take action on what you know is true and armor up.

Take a moment during your prayer time to truly reflect on which pieces of the armor of God need more equipping in your life. Ask God to help you understand those pieces more clearly and how to use them. Pray that He would help you fight battles through His strength and not your own. Ask God to help you be ready for the day when the battle comes your way.

HOW TO LIVE IN TRUTH

HOPEFULLY YOU'VE SEEN BY
NOW THAT TRUTH MATTERS.
BUT WE DON'T LEARN TRUTH
SIMPLY FOR ITS OWN SAKE—
WE LEARN THE TRUTH SO WE
CAN PUT IT INTO PRACTICE
AND LIVE IT OUT. AN ATHLETE
DOESN'T GO TO PRACTICE
AND PLAN TO NOT EVER PLAY
IN A GAME. IN THE SAME WAY,
WE GET TO LIVE OUT TRUTH
AND SEE WHAT IT LOOKS LIKE
IN OUR EVERYDAY LIVES.

TRUE WORSHIP

READ JOHN 4:1-26.

*"God is spirit, and those who worship
him must worship in Spirit and in truth."*
— John 4:24

DISCOVER

Everyone worships something. The fact is, humans were designed to
worship. Of course, we were designed to worship God, but many people
replace that true worship with a false worship. People worship celebrity,
power, pleasure, and many other things, all while God is calling them to
worship Him.

We only know who and how to worship because of the truth we find in
God's Word. The Bible reveals God's character and actions to us. We don't
worship based on what we think God is like; we worship based on who
God really is. It can be easy to allow worship to become an action that's
only about our emotions. Yes, our emotions do get involved in worship,
but never at the expense of the truth of who God is.

In today's Scripture reading, Jesus challenged the Samaritan woman to
understand that true worshipers are those who worship both in Spirit
and in truth. We must be given life by the Spirit, and we must learn the
truth about God by reading Scripture. The woman worried that worship
was about a place. She was concerned about which people had the right
location to worship. But worship is never about location because wherever
followers of Jesus gather, they can worship.

What do people sometimes get wrong about worship?

How can we focus on worshiping in Spirit and in truth?

DISPLAY

The worship that Jesus describes here isn't fake. It's not done for show. Worshiping in Spirit and truth is an act of authentic worship. You're alone by yourself right now. No one is judging you for how you worship. So, spend some time worshiping God. You might sing a song. Maybe say different characteristics of who God is out loud. Perhaps journal or write a poem that declares God's glory. No matter which direction you go, spend time worshiping Him. You'll find that your private times of worship make your public times of worship even better.

Use your prayer time to continue your time of worship. Praise Him for who He is. Thank God for what He has done in your life and in the lives of those you love. Sit quietly and allow yourself to be taken back by the beauty of the Lord.

AN APPROVED WORKER

READ 2 TIMOTHY 2:14-19.

Be diligent to present yourself to God as one approved, a worker who doesn't need to be ashamed, correctly teaching the word of truth.
— 2 Timothy 2:15

DISCOVER

A chainsaw in the hands of someone who's trained to use it is a powerful tool. This person can cut down trees, help clear debris, and perform a variety of other helpful tasks. A chainsaw in the hands of an untrained five-year-old kid, on the other hand, is a disaster waiting to happen. It's inevitable that this child is going to hurt himself, injure those around him, and destroy anything he comes into contact with.

Paul challenged Timothy to handle God's Word correctly. Timothy was to teach God's Word correctly and not to present it in a way that would lead to his shame. Paul pointed out others who had twisted God's Word and handled it without care. This led people astray, and the false teaching spread very quickly. People can even turn God's Word into a weapon when they use it the wrong way. Instead of spreading the good news of the gospel, mishandling God's Word can bring about false beliefs and fighting.

We all need to be serious about how we handle God's Word. We should respect it and acknowledge that it's literally how God has revealed Himself to us. The Almighty God of the universe is worthy of our reverence and respect. If we truly believe God is who He says He is, we should treat His Word in a way that honors Him.

Why is it so important to keep the main truths of the gospel at the center of our minds?

How can we be diligent as we engage with God's Word?

What are some core truths from the Bible that you see as critical for everyone to know?

80
LIFEWAY STUDENTS | DEVOTIONS

DISPLAY

Paul wrote these instructions with the idea in mind that Timothy needed to follow these as a pastor. But the guidelines here are not just for pastors. It's important for *all* believers to take their pursuit of God's Word seriously. Decide to become a student of the Bible—not in the sense of going to school but by choosing to go deeper than the surface when you read the Bible. Dig in and learn as much as you can. Commit to obey what you read. Ask good questions every time you approach the Scriptures.

In your prayer time, ask God to help you handle His Word the way He wants you to. Pray for wisdom as you read the Bible each day. Submit your own desires to whatever God has for you as you engage the Bible. Commit to obeying what you read and to help other people understand God's Word better as well.

TRUE VERSUS FALSE

READ PROVERBS 12:22.

Lying lips are detestable to the Lord, but faithful people are his delight.

DISCOVER

How do you feel when a friend lies to you? There aren't many feelings that are worse than finding out someone you trust has been saying things to you that are simply untrue or hiding things from you. We feel a sense of betrayal when we're lied to. We expect people to be honest and truthful with us.

Imagine how God, who is completely faithful and true, feels when He sees His creation lying. It's yet another mark of our fallen nature. It's another time when God's beautiful image that we've been created in is distorted into something other than what it was meant to be. God loves when people tell the truth. He wants people to tell the truth about Him, and He wants people to tell the truth when they speak about others.

All the way back in the beginning, God created a beautiful place and gave truth to His people. But from the very start, the enemy was a deceiver. He twisted the truth and misrepresented what God had said to the man and woman. God hates lying. He hates falsehood. That may sound harsh, but we must remember that God's hatred of lying shows His incredible love and affection for all that is true. We should hold this same view of truth and falsehood. We should delight in truth so deeply that it causes lying to look absolutely terrible in comparison.

Why does God hate lying lips?

Why does God delight in faithful people?

How should we respond to this proverb?

DISPLAY

God hates falsehood. As we seek to have this same heart and attitude, we ought to live this out in a couple of different ways. First, in ourselves: We should strive to tell the truth and stay far from lying. Second, we should encourage truth-telling in others around us. The way you approach that may be different depending on the person, but in all circumstances you can be a model of truthfulness and gently help people see that telling the truth is always better than telling lies. You can make a difference with your friends and family by building a culture that values telling the truth.

As you pray, thank God for being a God who is always truthful. He tells the truth one hundred percent of the time. Ask Him to give you that same heart. If lying has been a struggle for you, ask God to help you make changes in that area of your life. Commit to being a follower of Jesus who tells the truth to others.

DAY 24

TRUE LOVE

READ 1 CORINTHIANS 13.

Love finds no joy in unrighteousness but rejoices in the truth.
— 1 Corinthians 13:6

DISCOVER

There may have been situations in your life when you felt you were helping someone else by not telling them the truth. It may have been from good intentions: Maybe you thought this person's feelings would be hurt. Maybe you thought the person wouldn't know what to do. You may have even thought you were loving this person by lying to him or her or by withholding the truth.

The thirteenth chapter of 1 Corinthians is all about love. It's been read at many weddings (including mine) and is often referred to around Valentine's Day. But what it's really about is helping Christians understand what love looks like in the setting of worshiping together as a church community. We may think we are showing love by telling a "little white lie" to someone, but Paul tells us here that this is unloving. Real love doesn't find joy in unrighteousness. Biblical love finds incredible joy when the truth is told.

We often think of love as a warm, fuzzy, romantic feeling. But biblical love is about doing good toward others. And the best good for others is the truth. This doesn't always mean the truth is easy to hear. Sometimes the truth is difficult and can even hurt. But we can share truth in love with others with the aim of helping them grow and continually trust in God. This also means we need to be ready to receive truth from others who are talking to us with a motive of love. This, too, can be hard, but we can rejoice in the truth when others share it with us.

Which of the descriptions of love in this chapter stands out the most to you? Why?

How can Christians best love other believers in the church?

DISPLAY

Another way to look at the key verse for today is to evaluate whether you find more joy in what's wrong (unrighteousness) or in what's right (truth). It's easy to find ourselves sliding into finding joy in unrighteousness because we're surrounded by so much of it. Do a brief self-evaluation and ask yourself these questions: *Do I find more joy in what's wrong than what's right? Do I find myself laughing at entertainment that declares the opposite of God's truth? Do I ever contribute to this type of action in others?* If you find areas that need adjustment, repent and confess those to God.

Ask God to give you a better understanding of His love for you and ask Him how you can display His love to others. Pick one or two of the descriptions of love that you need to grow in and ask God for help in living them out better. Pray that He would give you opportunities to display biblical love to others.

TRUTH IN LOVE

READ EPHESIANS 4:11-16.

*But speaking the truth in love, let us grow
in every way into him who is the head — Christ.*
— Ephesians 4:15

DISCOVER

Church isn't a program you attend or some sort of spiritual show you watch—it's a family you belong to. One of the pictures the Bible uses for the church is a body. In Ephesians 4, Paul writes about how the different parts of the body help build up the rest of the body. This starts with the gifts God gives to different people and leaders in the church. These gifts are there to help the different people in the body (yes, including you) to be equipped to do the incredible work of ministry that is building up the whole body.

We do this work in all sorts of unique ways. It's one of the amazing things about the church. Some people build the body up in front of others and others do this behind the scenes. But everyone has a part to play. A key part of that building up is when we speak the truth in love. Some people are really great at speaking the truth, but they do so in a way that tears people down. This isn't very helpful.

We are called to bring the truth to others in the body of Christ. This can be challenging and scary to do sometimes. However, when the truth is spoken in love, it has a powerful effect on others and helps people and the church grow into who God wants them to be.

Take another look at the leadership gifts Paul describes in verse 11. How do you see these gifts in action in your local church?

Whose job is it to help build up the body: the leaders' or everyone's? Why do you think this?

What are some challenges to speaking the truth in love?

DISPLAY

Speaking the truth in love is tough. Here are a few ways to practice this: First, ask a trusted Christian friend if there's anything in your life he or she has seen and has wanted to confront you about but hasn't (I told you this was tough!). Second, be a person who shares the truth of God's Word in a loving way, even when it's tough. Maybe this means having a conversation with friends about God's truth in a way that's not angry or mean. Finally, take your time when you see the need to bring truth to a friend in a hard situation. God will give you the right words if you ask Him to.

Pray about two related things today: First, ask God to give you wisdom for when to share truth in love. Pray that He will give you the right words and attitude to share that truth. Second, ask God to help you be receptive when people share truth in love with you. Pray that He will help you receive it and not be defensive.

BEST DWELLING PLACE

READ PHILIPPIANS 4:4-9.

Finally brothers and sisters, whatever is true, whatever is honorable, whatever is just, whatever is pure, whatever is lovely, whatever is commendable — if there is any moral excellence and if there is anything praiseworthy — dwell on these things.
— Philippians 4:8

DISCOVER

Where do you dwell? It's not a word that we use a lot, but if you think about it for a second, you can probably come up with an answer. Your answer will probably be the address of the house or apartment you live in. You'd say you "dwell" there because it's the place where you spend most of your time. It's your home. It's the place where you live.

Just like our bodies have a place we dwell, our minds have an incredible capability to dwell in certain places. Our minds can dwell on mistakes we've made in the past. Our minds can dwell on a relationship we're in or wish we were in. Often, our minds dwell on all the things the world throws our way through entertainment, conversations with friends, and pop culture. This can lead us to feeling constantly anxious and distracted from the things of God.

Paul challenges us to dwell with our minds in a different place. He gives a full list of where to dwell, but the very first thing he mentions is truth. In a world where we are fed so many lies, we need to make the intentional effort to put truth at the center of our thoughts.

Look at verses 4-7 and jot down any commands you see Paul giving there. Which of those commands is the most challenging for you?

What are some practices you could adopt that would help you dwell on the things Paul mentions?

DISPLAY

How do we dwell on things that are true as well as the rest of the list Paul gives us? It starts with identifying some of the lies you may have been dwelling on previously. Create a list of lies you find your mind spending time on. After you've created this list, write a truth from God's Word next to each lie. Try to list a specific Bible verse that ties to that truth. Take a few minutes to dwell on the truths you just listed and reflect on how you can continue in them.

Use today's prayer time as a quiet time of reflection. Ask God to show you areas in your mind where you need to replace some lies with truth. Think deeply about Scriptures that reflect what Paul wrote about. Pray that God would help you learn to dwell on truth instead of lies.

MEMORY VERSE

FINALLY BROTHERS AND SISTERS, WHATEVER IS TRUE, WHATEVER IS HONORABLE, WHATEVER IS JUST, WHATEVER IS PURE, WHATEVER IS LOVELY, WHATEVER IS COMMENDABLE — IF THERE IS ANY MORAL EXCELLENCE AND IF THERE IS ANYTHING PRAISEWORTHY — DWELL ON THESE THINGS.

— Philippians 4:8

WALKING IN THE LIGHT

READ 1 JOHN 1:5-10.

If we say, "We have fellowship with him," and yet we walk in darkness, we are lying and are not practicing the truth.
— 1 John 1:6

DISCOVER

Imagine declaring you're a huge fan of a specific professional sports team. You talk about them all the time and how much you love them. You own multiple jerseys for that team's players and declare how great they all are. But then game day comes . . . and you cheer for the opponent when they score, instead. You even high five people around you when the opponent wins. Which team are you really a fan of?

In this letter, John writes about how it's impossible to declare you're in a relationship with Jesus and yet walk in a way that's the exact opposite of Him. God is light. Followers of Jesus walk in the light and not in the darkness. What does it mean to walk in darkness? Does it mean if we sin at all that we are walking in darkness? No. A person who walks in darkness is a person whose lifestyle shows a pattern of living in sin rather than living in the truth. Every Christian, while on this earth, still wrestles with sin and temptation. You will still sin as a Christian, even though you don't want to.

Our lives should reflect the person we say we are. We practice lies when we live a life that doesn't match the life of a follower of Jesus. Our aim should be to embrace the truth of who we are as Christians and pursue that with our whole hearts.

What are two things that result from walking in the light, according to verse 7? Why do you think these things are important?

Why is it important to admit that we sin?

What should our response be when we realize our sin (see v. 9)?

DISPLAY

Is there an area of your life where you've been flirting with darkness? Now is the time to deal with it. Conduct a heart check for yourself and see if there are areas where you have been veering off course. Decide today to ask the Holy Spirit to help you steer things back in the right direction. At the same time, make sure that you're not trying to somehow perform for God. Your actions don't save you; a trusting relationship with Jesus and in His work is what saves you. God will give you the strength you need as His son or daughter to follow Him.

In your prayer time, ask God to give you the strength to continue walking in the light. If there are areas where repentance is needed, take time to confess those sins to God and reaffirm your trust in His forgiveness. Commit in a fresh way to walk in the light.

YES = YES AND NO = NO

READ JAMES 5:12.

Above all, my brothers and sisters, do not swear, either by heaven
or by earth or with any other oath. But let your "yes" mean "yes,"
and your "no" mean "no," so that you won't fall under judgment.
— James 5:12

DISCOVER

We sometimes say things we don't mean. We make big promises that
we can't live up to. We get distracted and don't follow through on our
commitments. You may have a friend who says things like, "Let's hang out
this weekend." And you tell them that sounds great, but on the inside
you're thinking, "Yep, that's not going to happen."

People can get a bad reputation for not following through on what they
say. Don't be that type of person. James challenges us not to rise to
the level of making a big production out of an oath or swearing to do
something. We should simply be people who say what we mean and mean
what we say.

Maybe a friend asks you to help him with a school assignment over the
weekend but you really don't want to. What's your typical gut response?
You might say yes and not really want to. You might say yes because you
don't want to hurt your friend's feelings. James would encourage you to
say what you mean (with love and kindness).

Or maybe another friend asks you to go to her soccer game and you
really want to go. So you tell your friend you'll be there, but then you get
distracted with other things going on and you don't show up. James would
encourage you to follow through on what you say.

Why do you think James told people not to swear in this way?

What does it look like in real life to always let your "yes" mean "yes"?

Why do you think it's important to speak this way?

DISPLAY

Take some time to dig into why you might not live out this verse. Do you have trouble with telling people yes and not really meaning it? Perhaps slowing down on responding to people would be helpful. You could also respond differently when you need time to think about something. It's okay to say, "Let me get back to you." Do you have trouble with telling people yes and not following through with it? You might also need to slow down in this case, but the bigger need here may be to determine that you're going to be a person who follows through on your commitments.

As you pray today, ask God to help you be a person of your word. It's a mark of becoming like Jesus, so ask Him to help you grow into being more like Him in this way. Pray that God would shape you into a person who's truthful in all you words, including your commitments to others.

LOVE IN ACTION

READ 1 JOHN 3:13-18.

Little children, let us not love in word or speech, but in action and in truth.
— 1 John 3:18

DISCOVER

Talk is cheap. Actions speak louder than words. You've probably heard these sayings before. They may sound cliche, but they are true. Christians are really good at talking about things but not always very good at actually doing them. John gives several examples in today's verses. You can't have stepped into new life in Christ but not love your brothers and sisters. In the same way, you can't hate people and claim to have eternal life. You can't say you love people who are in need and then not be doing anything about it.

Love requires action. Love is not just a feeling or emotion—it's doing good toward others with their best interest in mind. We don't prove that we love others when we say we love them—we prove that we love them when we display it to them by our actions. The truth of our love is found in how we put it into practice.

A love without action is a halfway type of love. Halfway love tells your parents you love them as you walk out the door but doesn't take the trash out as they're always asking you to. Halfway love says you love your church but doesn't contribute by serving others in ministry. Halfway love tells your friends how much you care about them but then gossips behind their backs. God calls us to a love that shows up in action and truth, not just in our words.

According to John, what are some marks of someone who has passed from death to life? Why are these marks important?

Why do actions matter so much?

How has God displayed His love for us through His actions?

DISPLAY

Let's get really practical. Create a list of three ways you can display God's love to others. It might be through helping someone you know. It might be through participating in a service project. It might be through going the extra mile for someone in your life. Now that you've got a list, put it into action. Decide when you will do each action. Think about if you will complete it on your own or with some friends so they can have an opportunity to live out God's love as well. Give yourself a deadline to get it done, and then make it happen.

Spend time in prayer asking God to help you keep growing your love for Him and others into a love that is in action. Ask Him to show you opportunities throughout your day or week to put love into action. Thank Him for how He displayed His love for you by sending Jesus to die in your place and be raised from the dead.

YOU ARE NOT GOD

READ ISAIAH 55:8-11.

"For my thoughts are not your thoughts, and your ways are not my ways." This is the LORD's declaration.
— Isaiah 55:8

DISCOVER

Most of us have encountered a toddler who loves to ask "why?" No explanation seems to satisfy a three-year-old who wants to know why something is the way it is. This changes a bit as a we get older, but it's still there. As you entered your middle-school and high-school years, chances are that "why" became a big part of your vocabulary once again. Why do your parents have that rule? Why can't you stay out as late as you want? Why do you have to do chores?

I wish I could say it goes away, but even as an adult I still ask "why?" And sometimes it seems like things don't always get clearer as we follow Jesus. We don't always understand why God allows some things to happen. We can't get our brains around why things are the way they are. And then there's the reality that the Bible contains some things that are difficult to understand and accept. God's truth can seem at odds with how we view the world.

These verses in Isaiah help us see how to approach this situation. There are times when we just have to acknowledge that God is God and we are not. His thoughts aren't the same as ours. He knows better than us and we may not always be able to make sense of the "whys." Part of the process of growing in spiritual maturity is growing the ability to say, "I don't know, but I trust God anyways."

DELIGHT

What are some truths in Scripture that are difficult for you to understand? What makes them challenging for you?

If you could ask God one question, what would it be?

How do these verses encourage you to follow Jesus, even when you don't understand something?

DISPLAY

It's okay to have questions. It's okay to admit that you don't have everything figured out. Write down some things that are hard to understand from the Bible or that you find confusing. Find a time in the next few days to sit down with your parents, a pastor, or a youth leader you trust and talk through your questions. This adult may be able to help you understand better, or you might find an opportunity to still trust God with something that doesn't make sense to you.

Admit to God that He is God and you are not. This is a great way to start any time of prayer because it puts us in the right position before God. Share with Him about things that you struggle to understand. Ask Him to help you understand. Ask Him to give you the strength to trust Him with the big picture, even when the details don't make sense to you.

TELLING WHAT'S TRUE

When you were a kid, were there certain words you misspoke or things you understood incorrectly because you misinterpreted context clues? Maybe you thought a hamburger was made from ham. Or you heard "soup case" when someone said "suitcase." Maybe you believed that if you accidentally swallowed a watermelon seed, a watermelon would start growing in your stomach. Maybe an older sibling told you a story that scared you into sleeping with a nightlight, but it now seems silly.

As we grow, we learn the truth, and sometimes we look back and laugh at what we used to do, say, or believe as kids. But sometimes the truth is still difficult to determine, especially when the evidence or discovery is so cool or so unbelievable that we actually want it to be real.

Throughout history, widely believed hoaxes and the popularity of the internet have taught us not to believe everything we read or hear. Take a look at some of the wildest things people believed that turned out to be hoaxes, pranks, or nothing more than a poorly timed misunderstanding.

- **The Cardiff Giant:** A man had a ten-foot giant sculpture created and buried it on a relative's farm in New York. When a well was dug a few years later, the giant was "discovered." It became such a tourist attraction that P. T. Barnum created a replica to travel around the country, drawing lots of attention. People only lost interest as more replicas began to pop up across the country.

- **Bigfoot:** The first "evidence" of Bigfoot came from footprints created by a large wooden model of a foot that was made by a known prankster and stamped in the ground—all as a joke.

- ***War of the Worlds* Broadcast:** Some people weren't tuned into the radio station in time to hear the disclaimer that Orson Wells's *War of the Worlds* was a work of fiction, leading some to panic about an alien invasion.

- **Freeway Shark:** An image appeared of a shark viewed from a car window, swimming down the freeway after Hurricane Harvey. Ultimately, the photo was revealed as a fake that first surfaced after Hurricane Irene and can be tracked to a picture taken in 2005 in a National Geographic magazine.

- **Balloon Boy:** In 2009, parents called authorities saying their son was trapped in a homemade balloon that was shaped to look like a UFO. Eventually, the boy was found in the family's attic and admitted his dad set the whole thing up to try to get a reality TV show contract.

What are some hoaxes you've believed or fakes you've seen that look like the real deal?

We can all get sucked into lies because they seem to be true or we want them to be true. And because we're bombarded with information presented as truth online and on social media, it's tough to know where to turn for genuine truth. We all need an anchor, somewhere we can turn to discover truth when everything around us seems confusing and unsteady.

Thankfully, as we've seen over and over this past month, God is the source of truth. He is completely trustworthy; He can't lie, and He doesn't change. He is our unshakable anchor in an ever-changing world.

Read the following Scriptures and identify the images that show us what it means for us that God is stable, unshakable, trustworthy, and always in control.

- **Psalm 18:19; Psalm 31:8**
- **Psalm 23:1**
- **Psalm 27:1**
- **Psalm 46:3-11**
- **Psalm 47:6-7; Hebrews 1:3**
- **Psalm 62:1-2**
- **Proverbs 3:5-6**
- **Jeremiah 2:13; John 4:14**
- **Jeremiah 17:7-8**
- **James 1:17**
- **Mark 4:35-41**
- **Matthew 7:24-29**

After you read, choose a verse that stands out to you and do one of the following to represent the image depicted (river, mountain, crown, stronghold, etc.): (1) take a photo; (2) draw, paint, or create a sculpture; (3) print photos you find online or in magazines to create a collage below.

NOTES

UNWAVERING

Engage with God's Word.

lifeway.com/teendevotionals

☐ SEASONS

☐ FACING FEAR

☐ PRAYER

☐ IDENTITY

☐ SHAMELESS

☐ DISCONNECTED

☐ ETERNITY

☐ CHURCH

☐ SELFLESS

☐ BELONGING

☐ SET FREE

☐ INFLUENCER